Head St

GRADE 1

Contents

Editorial:
Laura Bourbonnais
Emmie Nicholson
Kaelan Ryan
Clarissa Sorgiovanni

Art Direction:
Doran Woo

Design:
Eleonora Fert
Viviane Machado
Doran Woo

Original Illustrations:
Steven Wood

Common Nouns

A **common noun** is a general name for a person, animal, place, or thing. Fill in the blanks using the examples provided. The first one is done for you.

Person

brother girl grandma

My grandma comes for dinner every Sunday.

Sarah has an older ______________ .

The ______________ is wearing a green dress.

Animal

parrot alpaca cat

The ______________ lives in the mountains.

My ______________ sleeps on my bed.

The ______________ has colourful feathers.

Place

space

island

forest

Bears and deer live in the _____.

There are many planets in _____.

We took a boat to the _____.

Thing

rocket

balloon

jam

The astronaut flies in a _____.

I like to put _____ on my toast.

I got a _____ at the carnival.

Can you come up with your own common nouns for each category?

Write each common noun from the word bank in the correct category.

book	**doctor**	**beach**	**glass**	**grape**	**mouse**
pig	**school**	**sister**	**store**	**turtle**	**uncle**

Person

Animal

Place

Thing

A **singular noun** names only one person, animal, place, or thing.

Examples: park bird tree friend

A **plural noun** names two or more persons, animals, places, or things. Most plural nouns are made by adding "s" to the singular noun.

Examples: parks birds trees friends

Circle the word that matches the picture.
The first one is done for you.

bee
bees

can
cans

plant
plants

pencil
pencils

bag
bags

star
stars

Some plural nouns are irregular, which means they don't end in "**s**." For example, the plural form of "tooth" is "teeth."

Proper Nouns

The names of your friends and family, your pets, and the city and country you live in are all proper nouns.

A **proper noun** names a specific person, animal, place, or thing and begins with a **capital letter**.

Circle the **proper nouns**. Write them correctly on the line below. The first one is done for you.

luna Luna	canada
ottawa	pillow
pear	jupiter
asia	mr. cruz
christina	pie

Replace the words in red with **proper nouns** of your choice. Write the new sentence on the line below. Remember to capitalize the **proper nouns**. The first one is done for you.

Proper Nouns

I feed my hamster every day.

I feed Max every day.

She came to my birthday party.

Last summer we went to the city.

I go to elementary school.

Today I walked home with my friend.

I visit the doctor for a checkup.

I like to pet the cat.

A **sentence** is a group of words that tells a complete thought. All sentences begin with a **capital letter** and end with a **punctuation mark**, such as a **period**.

Example: Pizza is my favourite food.

Is it a **sentence**? Circle thumbs up for "yes" and thumbs down for "no." The first one is done for you.

I love skateboarding.	👍 (circled) 👎
the lake.	👍 👎
and walk to it.	👍 👎
The car is red.	👍 👎
She put down the.	👍 👎
We had fun.	👍 👎

Draw a line to connect the groups of words that form sentences. The first one is done for you.

Fred and Lora are •	• berries.
Their greenhouse is •	• growing strawberries.
Fred waters •	• are red.
Lora picks the •	• the plants.
They work •	• together.
The strawberries •	• large.

Try coming up with your own endings to these sentences!

Use the word bank to finish each sentence.
Write the complete sentence on the line below.

astronaut | robot | fly | Bob | planets

My name is _______________.

____

I am an _______________.

____

I have a cool ________.

I explore ________.

Time to ________!

Questions

A question is an asking sentence. Questions often begin with one of the following words: "**who**," "**what**," "**where**," "**when**," "**why**," or "**how**."

Yes-or-no questions often begin with one of the following words: "**can**," "**is**," "**are**," "**do**," "**did**," or "**could**."

A **question** is a sentence that begins with a **capital letter** and ends with a **question mark** (?).

Example: **What is your favourite colour?**

Write each **question** correctly on the line below. The first one is done for you.

who is coming to the party

Who is coming to the party?

where is my backpack

did Sherin bring the basketball

when does class start

what month is it

how does it work

Is it a **question**?
Circle thumbs up for "yes" and thumbs down for "no."

I forgot my lunch box. 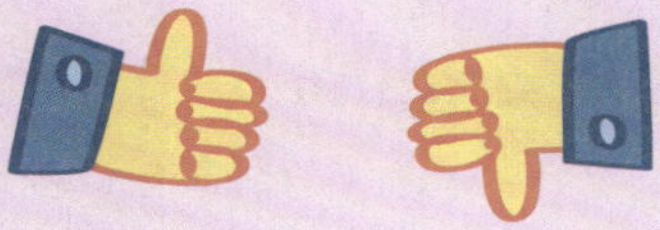

Can I play with you? 

The bicycle is purple. 

What did they say? 

Are you hungry? 

I am feeling sick. 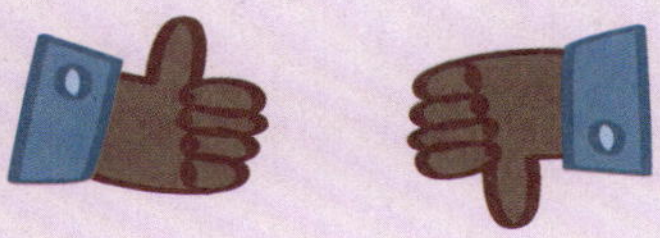

Can we keep it? 

Try writing your own question for Izzy the Iguana. For example, "What do you eat?"

Exclamatory Sentences

What kind of facial expressions do you think you might make when saying an exclamatory sentence? Make a different facial expression for each sentence on this page.

An **exclamatory sentence** shows strong feelings such as love, surprise, and fear. Exclamatory sentences start with a **capital letter** and end with an **exclamation mark** (!).

Example: **What a surprise!**

Is it an **exclamatory sentence**? Circle thumbs up for "yes" and thumbs down for "no." The first one is done for you.

That's so funny! (thumbs up circled)

I do not like mushrooms.

Did you drink water?

The movie was so cool!

He ate the last piece!

Exclamatory Sentences

Write each **exclamatory sentence** correctly on the line below. The first one is done for you.

you scared me

You scared me!

that car is so fast

she's the winner

wow, that's beautiful

ah, there's a spider

i can't wait

i forgot my bag

Capital Letters

A sentence begins with a **capital letter**. Proper nouns and the pronoun "I" are also **capitalized**.

Write each sentence correctly on the line below.
The first one is done for you.

my dog oliver is brown.

My dog Oliver is brown.

we went on a trip to ontario.

ana is from mexico.

bree and kai played jenga.

i like eating at taco bell.

we camped in banff park.

jane and i shop at costco.

Holidays, months of the year, and days of the week begin with **capital letters**.

Write each word from the word bank correctly in the right box. The first one is done for you.

january | labour day | monday | june | tuesday | easter

Holidays

Easter

Months of the Year

Days of the Week

Write each sentence correctly on the line below.

this wednesday is christmas!

my birthday is august 16.

i have art class on tuesday.

Capital Letters

Words such as "birthday" and "anniversary" are not capitalized because they are not proper nouns. However, specific holidays such as "Ramadan" and "New Year's Eve" are!

A sentence always ends with a **punctuation mark**.
A **statement sentence** tells what someone or something is doing. A statement sentence ends with a **period**.

Example: **Her hair is brown.**

A question ends with a **question mark**.

Example: **Are you ready?**

An exclamatory sentence ends with an **exclamation mark**.

Example: **I forgot my pencil!**

Add the proper punctuation to the end of each sentence. The first one is done for you.

When did Peter arrive ?

Jen planted seeds in the garden ____

Would you like to play with me ____

I wore my new shoes to school ____

Yay! Mikayla brought cake ____

We're going to be late ____

A **comma** (,) is used to separate items listed in a sentence.

Example: **She brought cake, cupcakes, and muffins to the bake sale.**

Add commas to separate the items in each sentence.

Brianna Jeremy and Lily are my cousins.

My favourite hobbies are drawing playing football and swimming.

I have hockey practice on Monday Wednesday and Friday.

I used green blue and yellow crayons to draw.

Do you want chocolate vanilla or strawberry ice cream?

I want pepperoni cheese and peppers on my pizza.

We are travelling to Toronto Ottawa and Montreal.

I live with my mom my dad and my sister.

Punctuation

Commas are only used to separate items when there are three or more items in a list. For example, this sentence does not need a comma: "I like blue and red."

A **verb** is an action word that describes what someone or something is doing.

Examples:

Sam drives his truck.

The dog steals my socks.

Nathan jumps.

Circle the verbs. The first one is done for you.

read	bucket	dance	cute	paper	talk
pink	swim	blue	car	run	play
Bailey	eye	climb	mouse	sing	why

Use the word bank to fill in the missing **verbs**.

ride eats dives

Katie ______________ her ice cream.

I ______________ my bicycle.

Victor ______________ into the pool.

Is the underlined word a **verb**? Circle thumbs up for "yes" and thumbs down for "no." The first one is done for you.

The kids play together.

Anna gives Max her bunny.

He loves his toy car.

They make a mess.

Anna and Max draw.

On the sentences you circled "no" for, underline the correct verb.

Subjects

The **subject** of a sentence is who or what the sentence is about.

Examples:

Tina threw the ball.

The puppies ran across the lawn.

Circle the subject in each sentence.
The first one is done for you.

My brother has green eyes.

Last year, I won the science fair.

My family walked in the park.

The cat is snuggled in its bed.

The mug is full of tea.

Walter went to the movies.

Use the word bank to fill in the missing **subjects**.
The first one is done for you.

birds | Hugo | twins | sister | Emma

My sister brushes her teeth.

_____ walks his dog.

The _____ sing.

The _____ love to read.

_____ waters the flowers.

Pronouns

We can use pronouns to replace nouns when the reader or listener already knows who or what we are talking about.

For example: "Did you see the movie? It was so good!" In the second sentence, "it" is used to replace "the movie."

Pronouns are words such as "she," "he," "they," "it," and "you" that can take the place of a noun.
Draw a line to match the words to the correct **pronoun**.
The first one is done for you.

Steven and Mike •	• we
the boy •	• it
the cat •	• he
Diana and I •	• they
The girls •	• he
Sally •	• we
Alan •	• it
The chair •	• you
You and I •	• they
You and Aileen •	• she

An **adjective** is a word that describes a noun. It might describe the colour, size, number, taste, texture, temperature, sound, or shape of a noun.

Examples:

The mango is sweet.

The two sweaters were silky.

crunchy | new | fluffy | salty | cold

The popsicle is __________ .

The panda is __________ .

I love my __________ bicycle helmet.

The peanuts are __________ and __________ .

What adjectives describe you? Are you tall, short, old, young, funny, shy, happy, or sleepy?

Write down two **adjectives** that describe each picture.

Sight Words

Sight words are common words that you can recognize right away without having to sound them out.

What colour is each picture? Write the answer on the line below. The first one is done for you.

green | black | orange | brown

yellow | blue | red | purple

red

Find the following sight words in the word search puzzle.

ABOUT	EVERY	MANY
AFTER	FROM	PLAY
COULD	HELP	THEIR
DOWN	HERE	WITH

F	R	O	M	M	A	N	Y	H	I
W	K	W	I	E	B	N	I	E	V
O	M	I	F	A	O	C	V	L	F
A	F	T	E	R	U	U	E	P	W
J	B	H	L	T	T	P	L	A	Y
E	H	D	O	A	R	O	V	S	T
V	X	J	S	U	U	B	R	K	H
E	H	E	R	E	C	G	M	W	E
R	T	W	G	J	D	O	W	N	I
Y	C	O	U	L	D	P	W	Y	R

Vocabulary

Practice writing each word then find it in the word search puzzle.

bowl 

chair 

cup 

fork 

pan 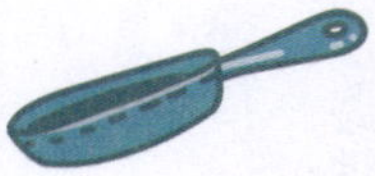

pot 

sink 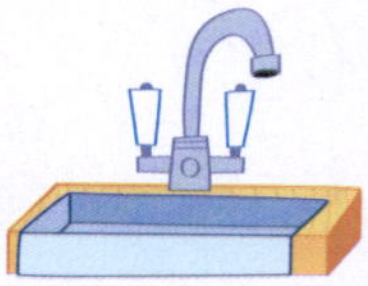

spoon 

table 

Y	A	H	J	N	W	C	N	F	P	D
D	X	P	Z	J	P	I	B	O	O	T
Y	Z	D	W	H	C	O	I	R	C	X
E	P	W	F	U	A	X	P	K	U	P
Y	A	L	S	J	T	A	B	L	E	O
V	N	M	D	S	S	P	O	O	N	T
P	C	H	A	I	R	P	N	C	U	P
G	T	R	T	N	S	R	V	U	M	I
B	O	W	L	K	D	P	E	R	N	T

Practice writing each word then find it in the word search puzzle.

black **blue** **brown**

green **orange** **pink**

purple **red** **yellow**

A	I	D	T	U	P	V	V	R	M	X
R	T	V	G	T	M	N	E	D	D	P
B	R	O	W	N	R	U	J	U	C	U
L	M	N	G	R	E	E	N	Y	O	R
A	S	W	G	S	I	Y	O	U	R	P
C	B	Y	E	L	L	O	W	R	A	L
K	L	H	S	U	Z	O	E	B	N	E
D	U	P	I	N	K	L	H	Q	G	X
R	E	D	E	H	P	G	J	X	E	W

Practice writing each word then find it in the word search puzzle.

bear

bird

cat

cow

dog

duck

fish

lion

koala

E	H	K	U	W	U	X	U	Z	Q	B
K	J	R	G	A	X	M	T	C	A	T
A	H	B	E	F	G	T	B	O	O	T
F	D	B	V	B	I	R	D	W	D	T
G	V	E	D	Z	F	W	P	F	U	U
K	I	A	E	F	I	S	H	P	C	T
V	O	R	B	I	Z	Z	Y	D	K	X
M	H	L	G	L	I	O	N	H	S	V
K	O	A	L	A	F	Q	C	D	O	G

Practice writing each word then find it in the word search puzzle.

bike 

boat 

bus 

car 

feet 

plane 

scooter 

train 

truck 

K	Q	C	Q	B	I	K	E	H	Y	Z
X	P	C	W	Q	P	K	C	J	S	T
T	R	A	I	N	Z	L	P	S	C	M
X	T	F	L	L	L	A	L	V	O	C
T	R	U	C	K	B	C	A	R	O	S
P	F	H	T	E	O	V	N	W	T	B
M	E	T	F	F	A	Q	E	S	E	U
V	E	Y	P	X	T	Y	L	Q	R	S
O	T	F	H	V	O	J	O	Y	B	P

Count the animals in each group and write the number in the box.

Why are fish so smart?

Because they swim in schools!

Count the items in each group and write the correct number word on the line. The first one is done for you.

one two three four five

six seven eight nine ten

six

Counting

What is the largest group on these two pages? What is the smallest group?

Count the items in each group and circle the correct number below.

10 12 14

14 11 13

12 11 10

15 16 17

Count the items in each group and circle the correct number below.

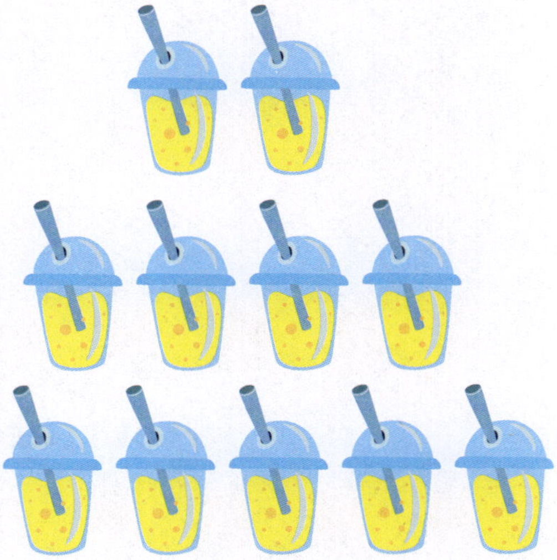

11 13 15

17 10 12

10 16 13

15 20 18

Counting

Draw a line to connect each number to the correct number word. The first one is done for you.

14	ten
2	seven
10	fourteen
12	eight
20	sixteen
7	two
16	twenty
11	twelve
8	eleven

Do these number words match the numbers? Put check marks beside the ones that match and fix the ones that don't. The first ones are done for you.

twelve	21	12	twenty	20	
seventeen	17	✓	nine	9	
ten	1		sixteen	61	
eleven	11		nineteen	91	
eighteen	81		fourteen	14	

Print the numbers that come before or after. The first one is done for you.

1	2			14		8	
	25		22			29	
35		37		43	44		
	49	50		22			

Keep a number line or a ruler handy to get used to large numbers. You can refer to it while completing this activity.

Counting

Skip counting is when we count by multiples of a number (such as **2**, **5**, **10**, or **50**) instead of counting **1** at a time. It helps you count to a large number more quickly!

Connect the dots, counting by 10s. Then colour the picture!

Look at the images shown on this spread. Read the questions and write your responses in the boxes.

How many eyes do you see? ☐

How many frames? ☐

How many stars? ☐

What do aliens like to read?

Comet books!

Look at the image shown on this spread. Read the questions and write your responses in the boxes.

How many balloons do you see? ☐

How many stars? ☐

How many hearts? ☐

Connect the dots, counting by 5s.

Connect the dots, counting by 2s.

Count the items in each group and write the number in the box below. Write the sum in the last box. The first one is done for you.

3 + 2 = 5

☐ + ☐ = ☐

☐ + ☐ = ☐

☐ + ☐ = ☐

☐ + ☐ = ☐

Write each sum this way too!

	3
+	2
	5

	☐
+	☐
	☐

	☐
+	☐
	☐

	☐
+	☐
	☐

	☐
+	☐
	☐

Count the items in each group and write the number in the box below. Write the sum in the last box.

☐ + ☐ = ☐

☐ + ☐ = ☐

☐ + ☐ = ☐

☐ + ☐ = ☐

Write each sum this way too!

Why did the banana go to the doctor?

Because he wasn't *peeling* well!

Write the numbers shown on each domino and find the sum.
The first one is done for you.

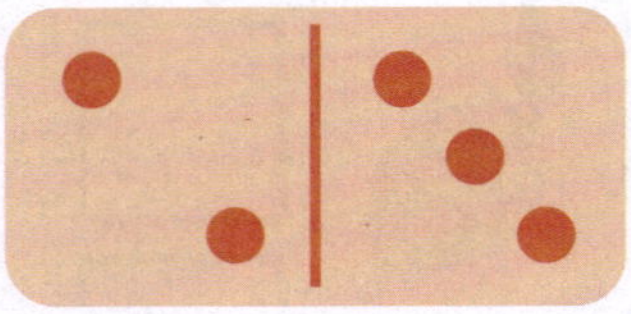

2 + 3 = 5

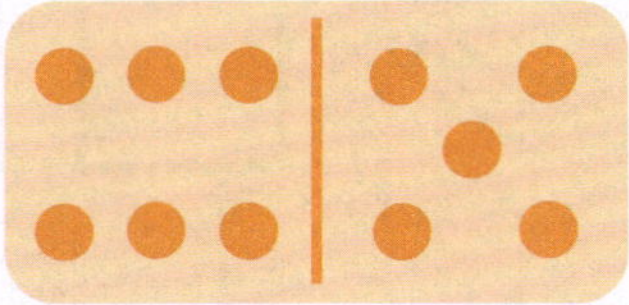

☐ + ☐ = ☐

☐ + ☐ = ☐

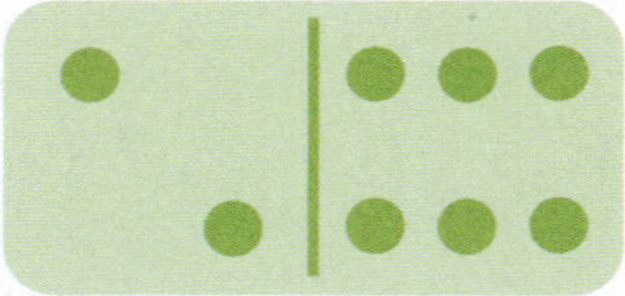

☐ + ☐ = ☐

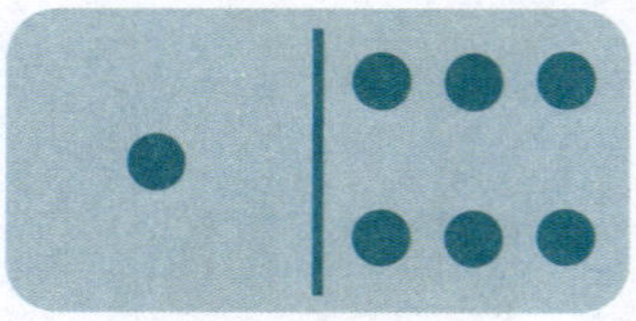

☐ + ☐ = ☐

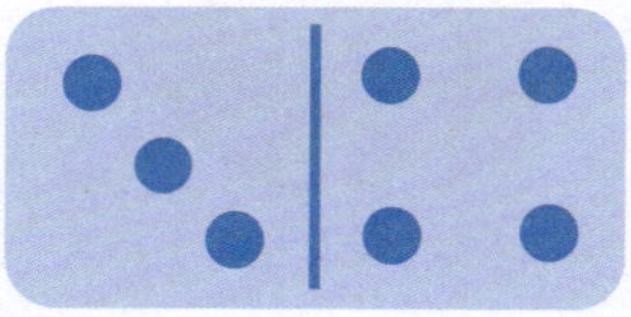

☐ + ☐ = ☐

Write the numbers shown on each domino and find the sum.
The first one is done for you.

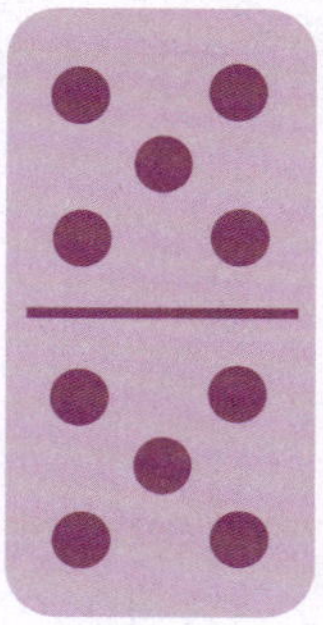

5
\+ 5
10

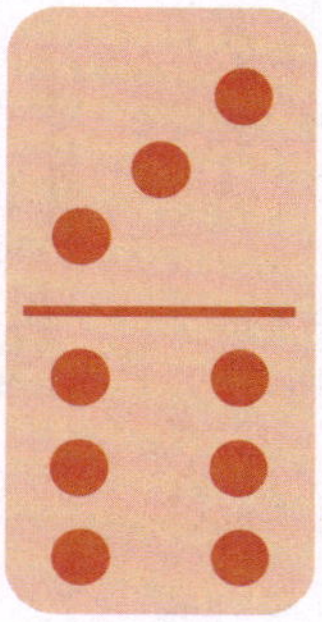

\+

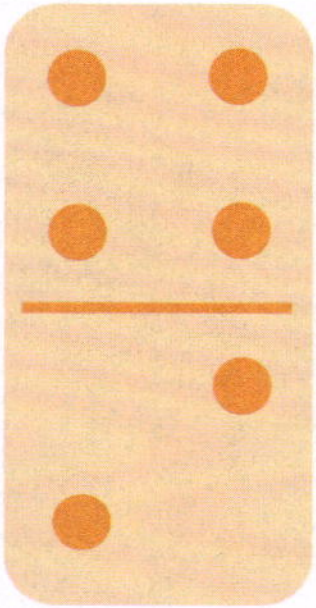

\+

\+

\+

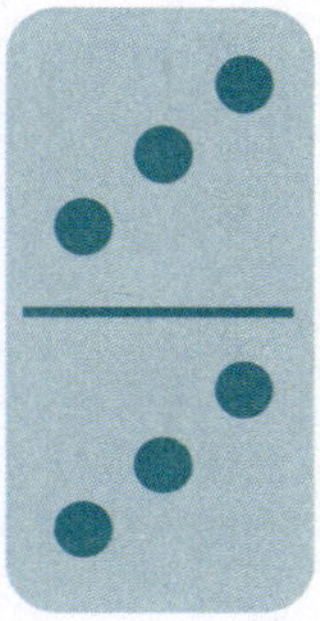

\+

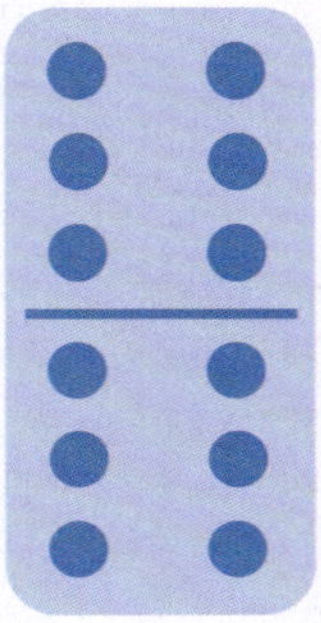

\+

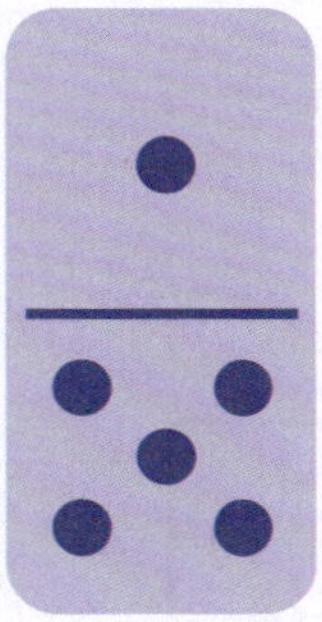

\+

Use the number line to help you add.

Example: 2 + 4 = ?

Answer: 2 + 4 = 6

1 + 1 = ☐

1 + 2 = ☐

1 + 3 = ☐

1 + 4 = ☐

1 + 5 = ☐

1 + 6 = ☐

1 + 7 = ☐

1 + 8 = ☐

1 + 9 = ☐

1 + 10 = ☐

2 + 1 = ☐

2 + 2 = ☐

2 + 3 = ☐

2 + 4 = ☐

2 + 5 = ☐

2 + 6 = ☐

2 + 7	2 + 8	2 + 9	10 +10	3 + 3
4 + 3	5 + 3	6 + 3	7 + 3	8 + 3
10 + 4	8 + 4	6 + 4	4 + 4	7 + 4
9 + 4	8 + 4	7 + 9	6 +10	10 + 3

The easiest way to add is by starting with the bigger number and adding the smaller number. For example, to solve **3 + 5**, begin at **5** and count up **3** more.

Subtraction

The solution will be the number of items in the group that are not crossed out.

Count the items in each group and write the number in the box below. Write the difference in the last box. The first one is done for you.

5 - 2 = 3

[ ] - [ ] = [ ]

[ ] - [ ] = [ ]

[ ] - [ ] = [ ]

Write each difference this way too!

	5
−	2
	3

−	

−	

−	

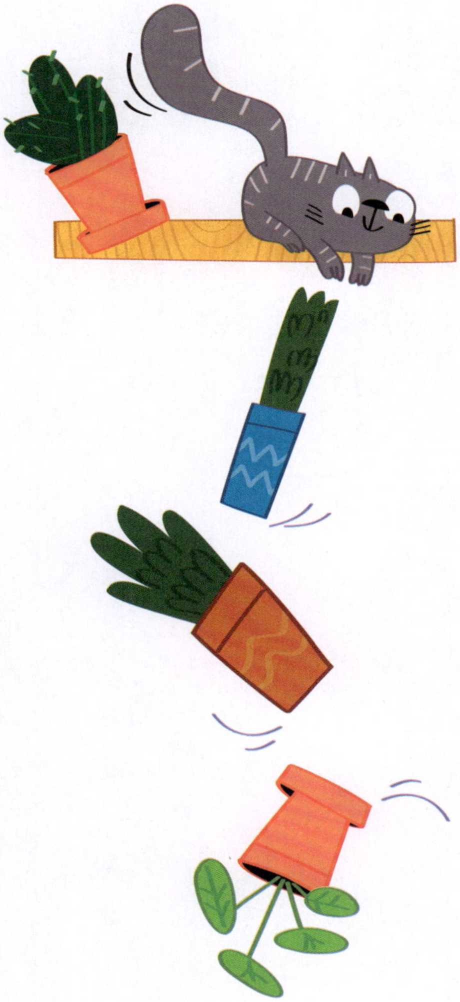

Count the items in each group and write the number in the box below. Write the difference in the last box.

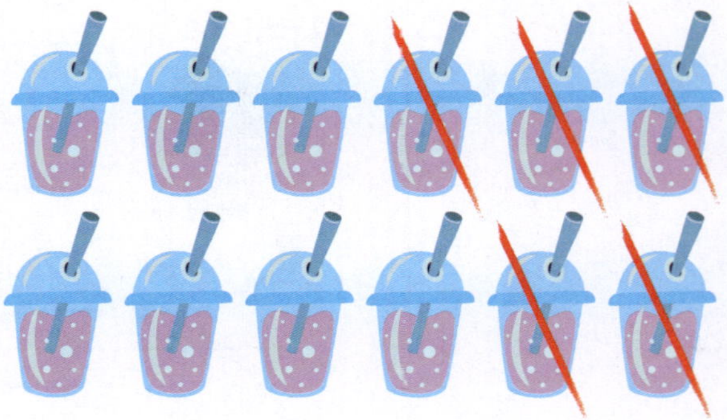

□ - □ = □

□ - □ = □

□ - □ = □

Write each sum this way too!

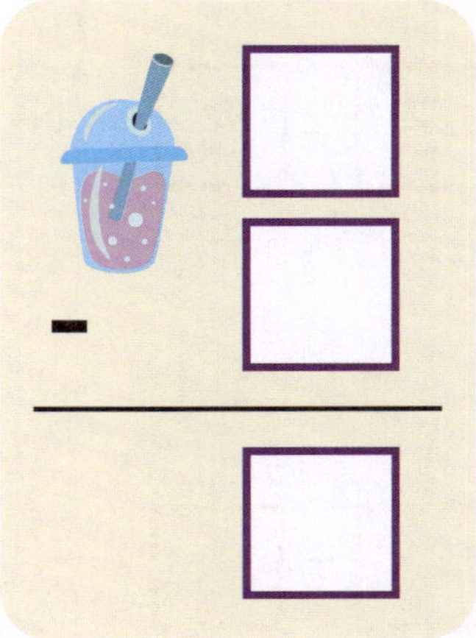

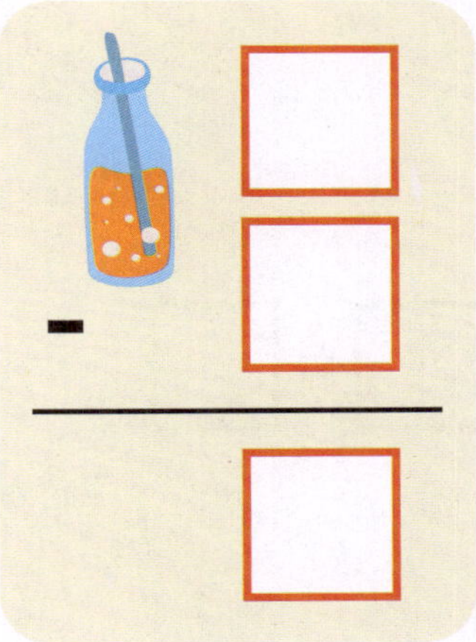

Subtraction

The dots on a domino are called "pips"!

There are many fun games you can play with a set of dominoes.

Write the numbers shown on each domino and find the difference. The first one is done for you.

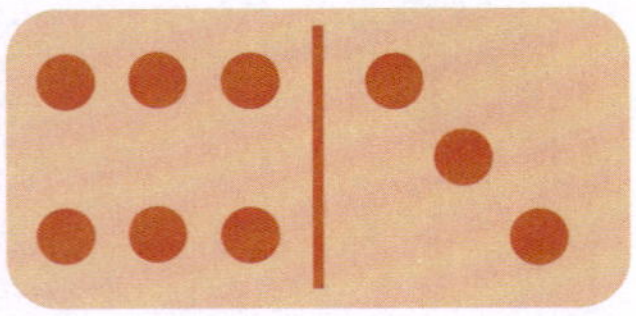

$6 - 3 = 3$

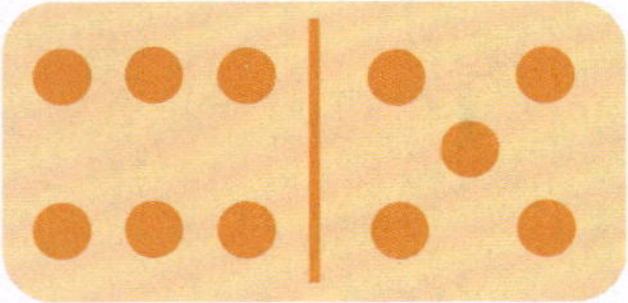

$\square - \square = \square$

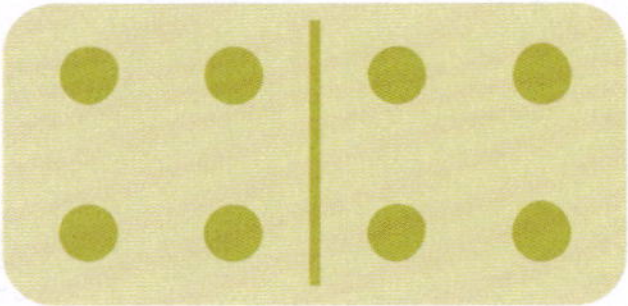

$\square - \square = \square$

$\square - \square = \square$

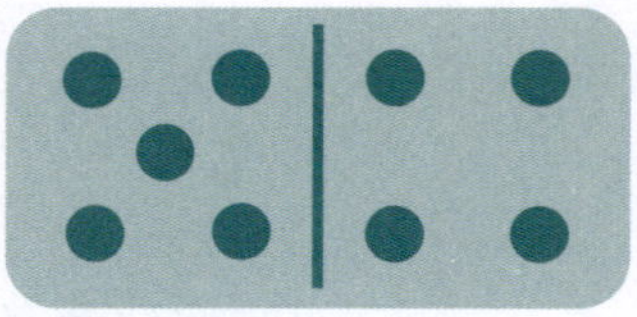

$\square - \square = \square$

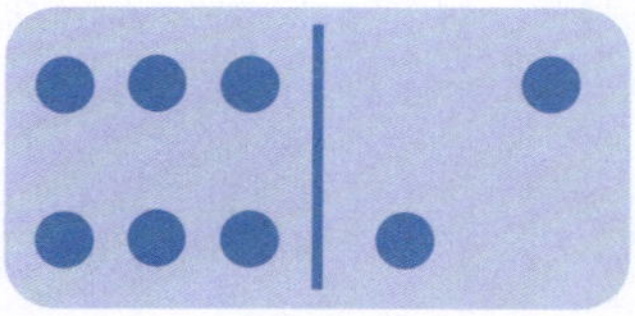

$\square - \square = \square$

Write the numbers shown on each domino and find the difference. The first one is done for you.

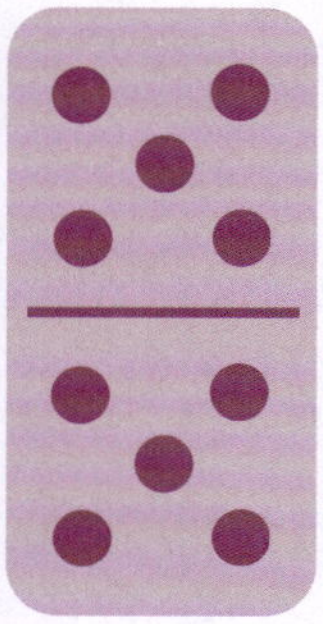

$$\begin{array}{r} 5 \\ -\ 5 \\ \hline 0 \end{array}$$

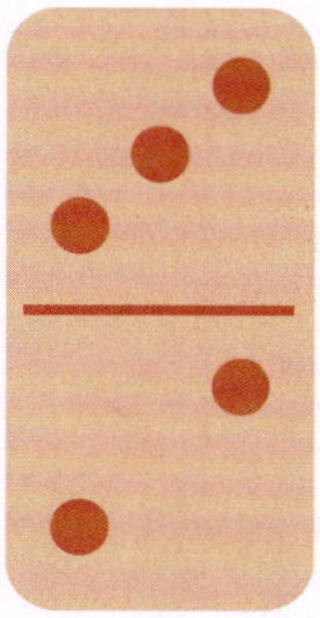

$$\begin{array}{r} \square \\ -\ \square \\ \hline \square \end{array}$$

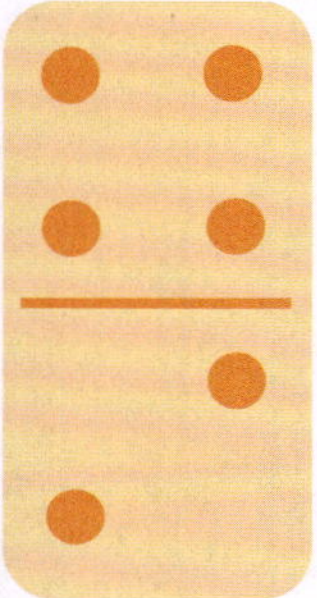

$$\begin{array}{r} \square \\ -\ \square \\ \hline \square \end{array}$$

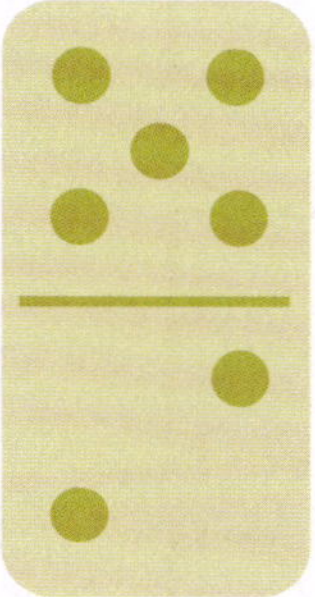

$$\begin{array}{r} \square \\ -\ \square \\ \hline \square \end{array}$$

$$\begin{array}{r} \square \\ -\ \square \\ \hline \square \end{array}$$

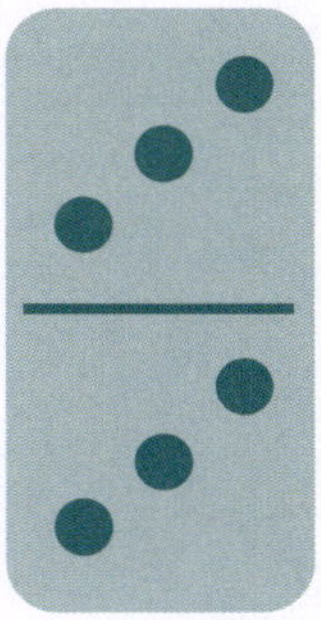

$$\begin{array}{r} \square \\ -\ \square \\ \hline \square \end{array}$$

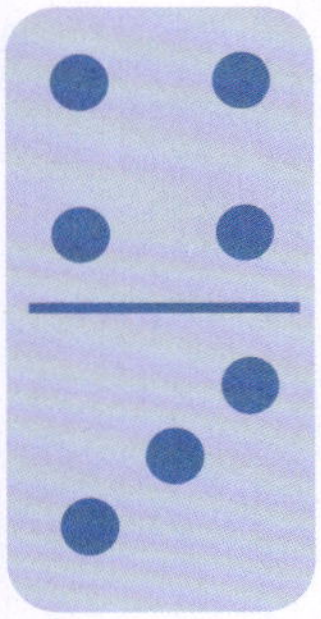

$$\begin{array}{r} \square \\ -\ \square \\ \hline \square \end{array}$$

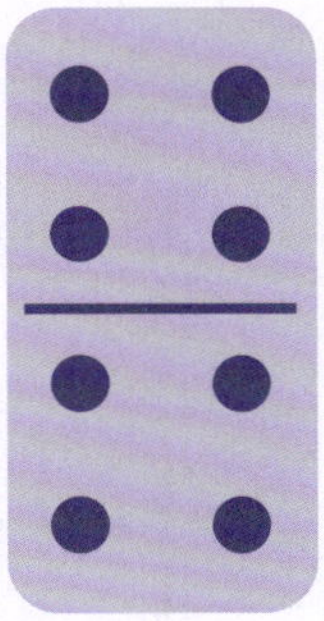

$$\begin{array}{r} \square \\ -\ \square \\ \hline \square \end{array}$$

Use the number line to help you subtract.

Example: 19 - 4 = ?

Answer: 19 - 4 = 15

6 - 1 =	10 - 3 =
7 - 2 =	10 - 6 =
8 - 3 =	10 - 2 =
5 - 4 =	10 - 4 =
5 - 3 =	10 - 1 =
9 - 1 =	10 - 5 =
8 - 2 =	10 - 10 =
6 - 3 =	10 - 0 =

15	15	15	15	15
- 8	- 1	- 9	- 3	- 6
□	□	□	□	□

20	20	20	20	20
- 9	- 2	- 8	- 5	-10
□	□	□	□	□

18	18	18	18	18
- 5	- 4	- 3	- 2	- 1
□	□	□	□	□

12	16	11	17	19
- 7	- 6	- 5	- 4	- 3
□	□	□	□	□

If you subtract **0** from a number, the number doesn't change. For example, **5 - 0 = 5**.

Adding **0** to any number has the same result! **5 + 0 = 5**.

Circle the **smaller** one.

Circle the **bigger** one.

Circle the ones that are the **same** size.

Draw a **smaller** carrot.

Draw a **bigger** flower.

Draw a **bigger** mushroom.

Draw a **smaller** pear.

Draw a **smaller** donut.

Draw a **bigger** star.

Draw a banana that is the **same** size.

Draw an apple that is the **same** size.

Relative Size

If an item is taller, it means that it is bigger vertically (top to bottom). If an item is longer, it means that it is bigger horizontally (left to right).

Circle the **taller** one.

Circle the **longer** one.

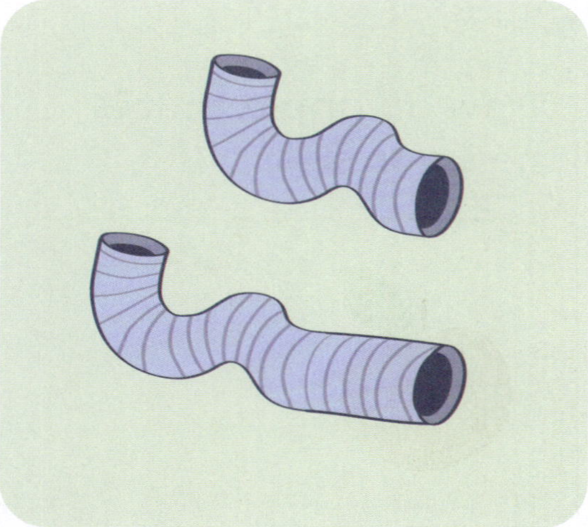

Colour the **taller** one.

Colour the **longer** one.

Circle the **heavier** one.

Circle the one that **holds more**.

Colour the **heavier** one.

Colour the one that **holds more**.

Add the numbers missing from the clock faces.

Add the numbers missing from the clock faces.

Telling Time

There are 12 hours on a clock face but 24 hours in a day. How can that be?

The hour hand goes around the clock twice per day: once for a.m. (the morning) and once more for p.m. (the afternoon and evening).

Telling Time

The number the little hand is pointing to tells what hour it is! For example, if the little hand is pointing at the 3, it is 3:00.

Tell the time to the hour. The first one is done for you.

4 o'clock

☐ o'clock

☐ o'clock

☐ o'clock

☐ o'clock

☐ o'clock

Tell the time to the half hour. The first one is done for you.

8:30

:

:

:

:

:

The big hand tells the minute. There are 60 minutes in an hour.

When the big hand points up at the 12, it is 0 minutes past the hour. When it points down at the 6, it is 30 minutes (half) past the hour.

Draw the hands on the clock to show the time.
The first one is done for you.

3:00

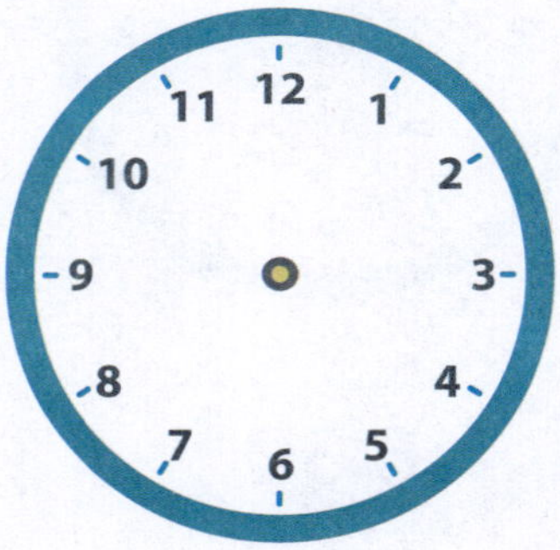

11:00

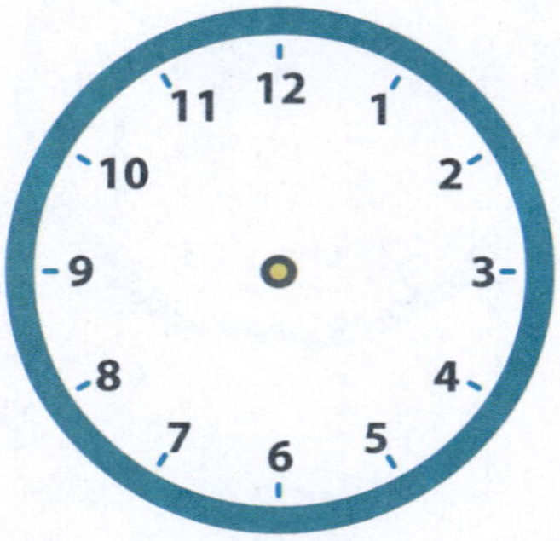

8:00

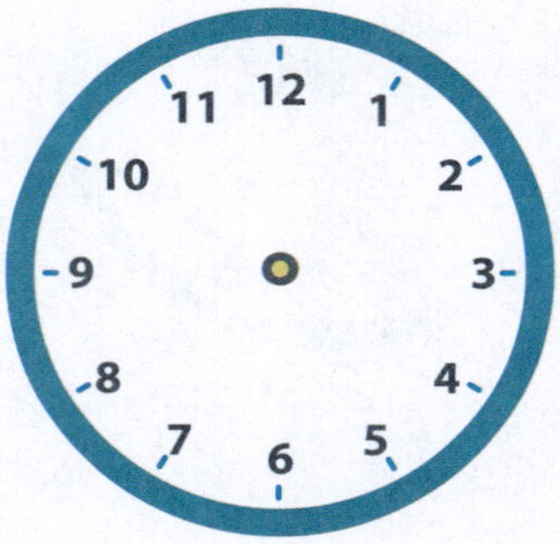

12:00

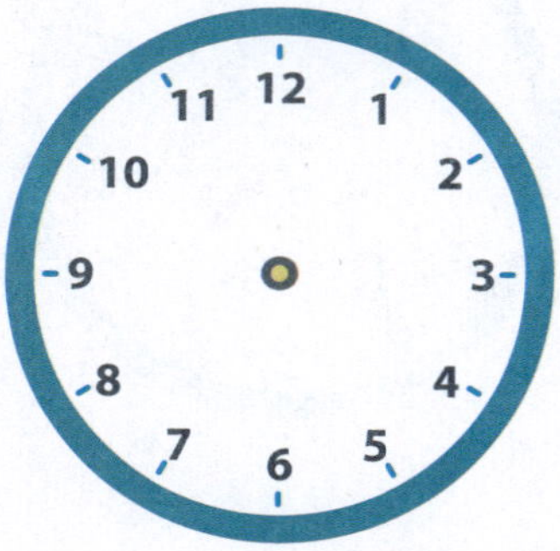

6:00

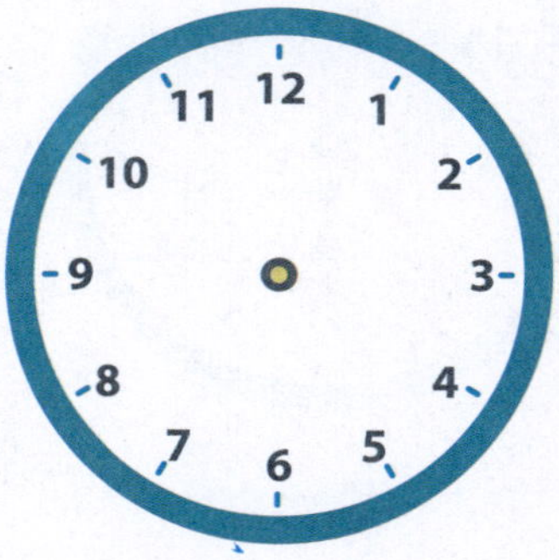

5:00

3:30

1:30

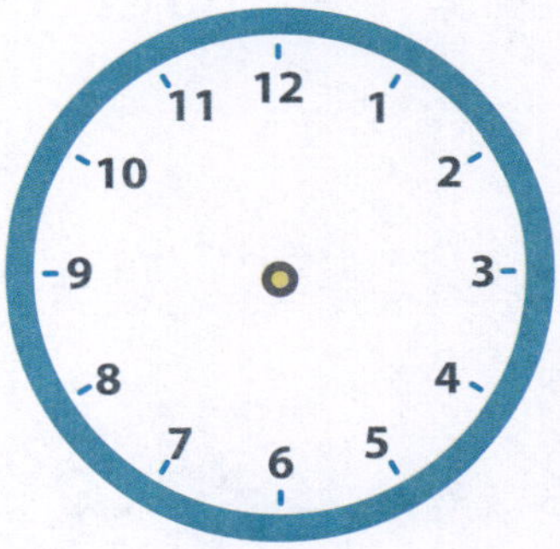

8:30

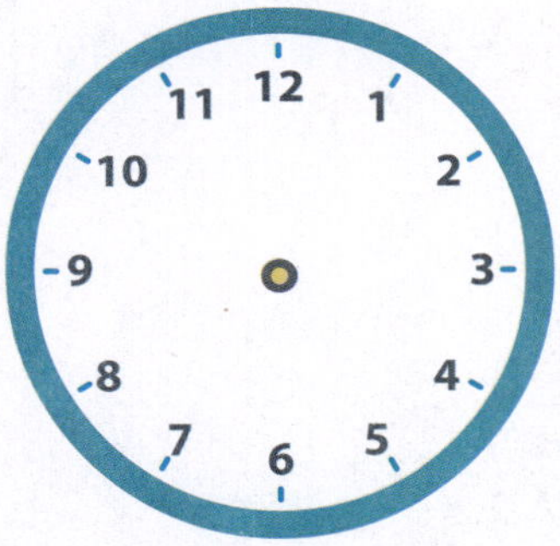

12:30

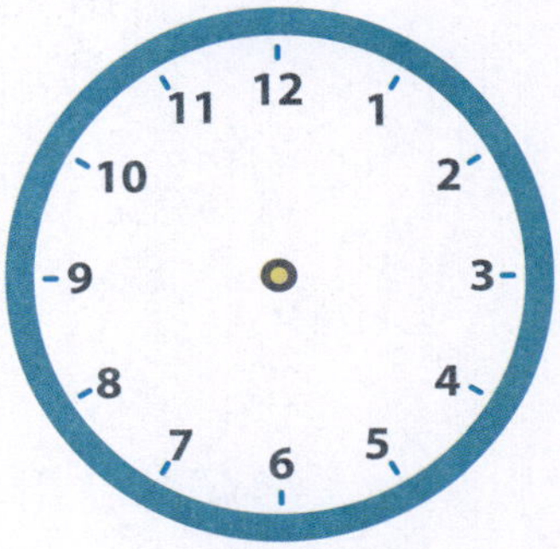

10:30

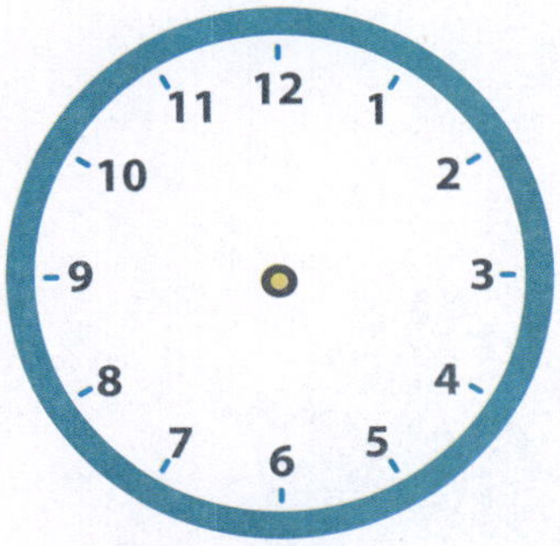

5:30

How many sides does each shape have? Which shape has the most sides? Which shapes have none?

Draw lines to connect the shapes to their names.

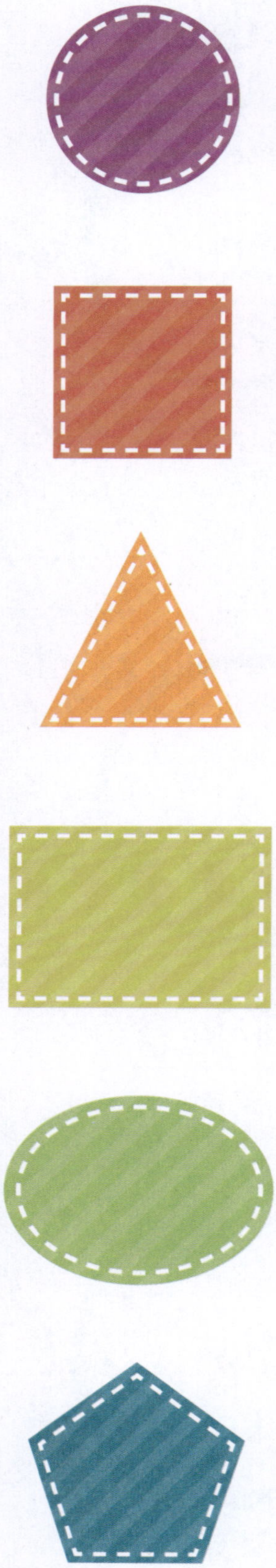

- triangle
- oval
- square
- pentagon
- circle
- rectangle

Draw each shape on the grid. The first one is done for you.

square
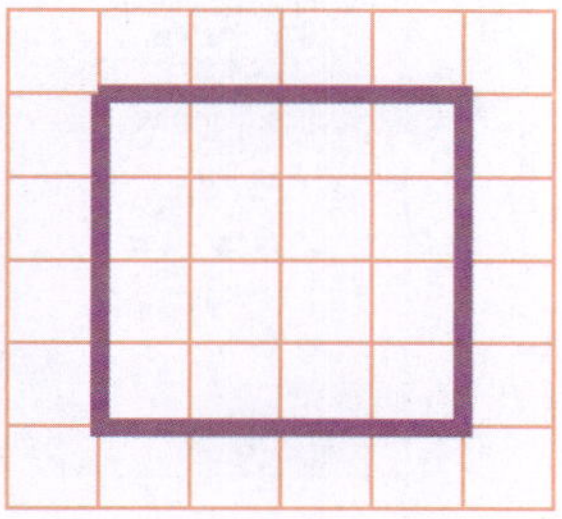

triangle
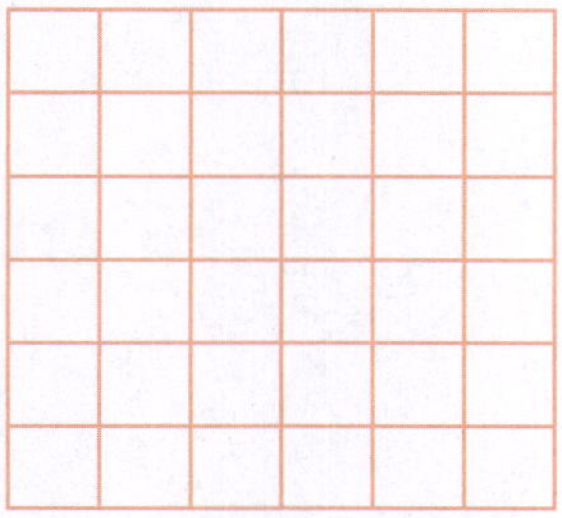

rectangle
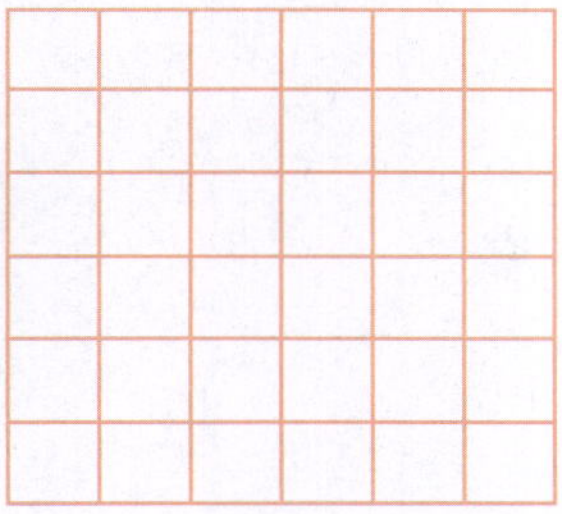

diamond
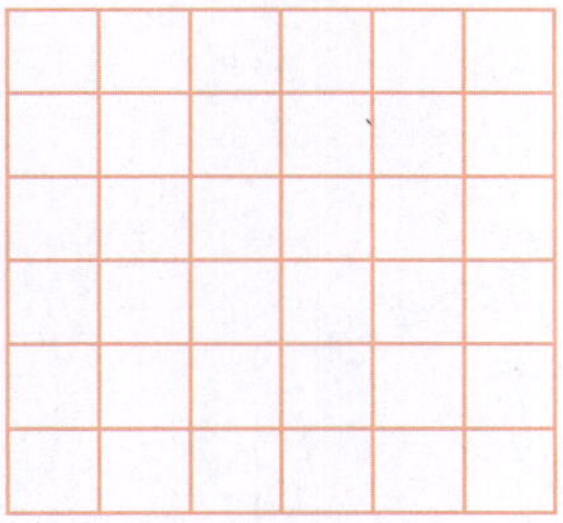

pentagon
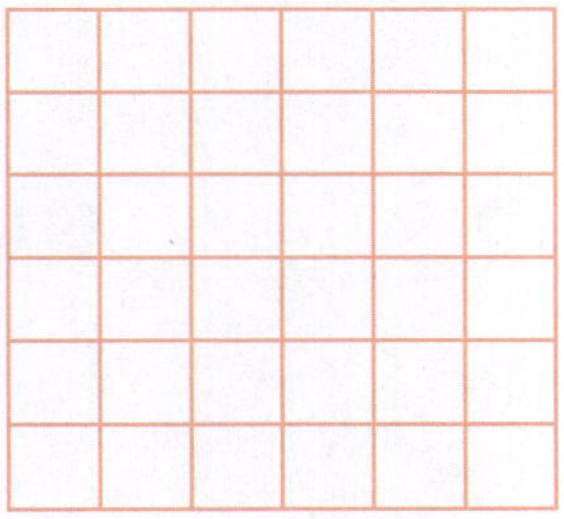

circle
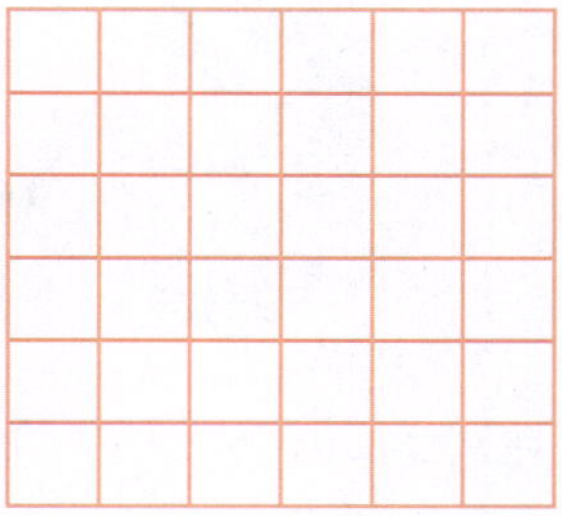

heart
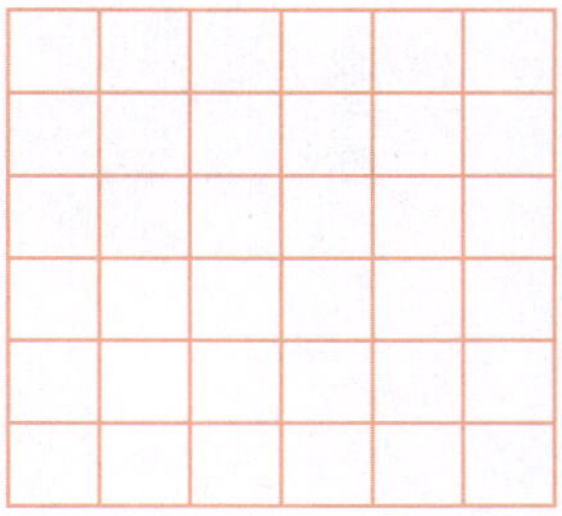

star
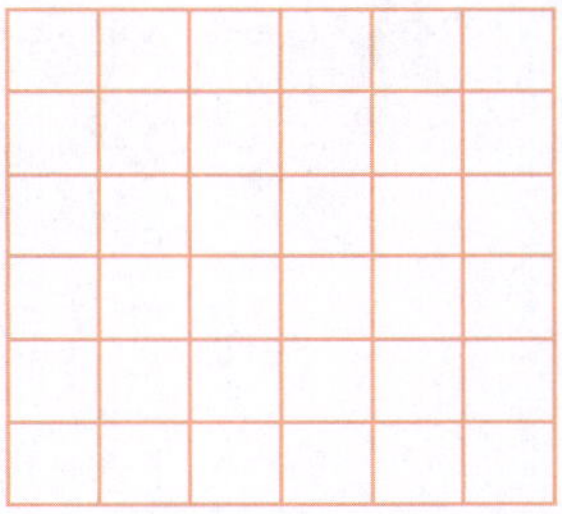

oval
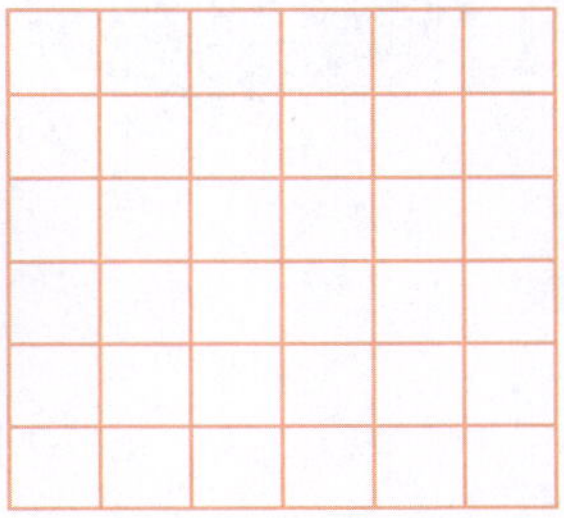

Draw lines to connect the 3D shapes to their names.

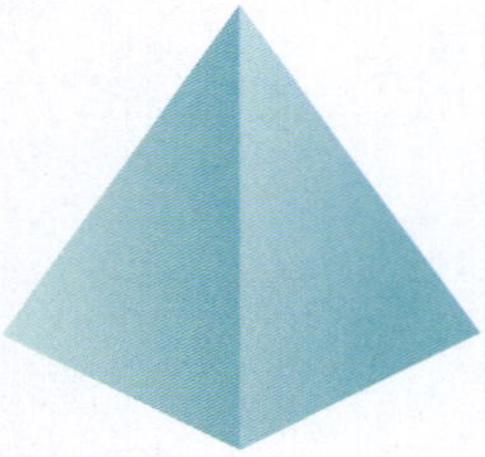 cylinder

 cone

 pyramid

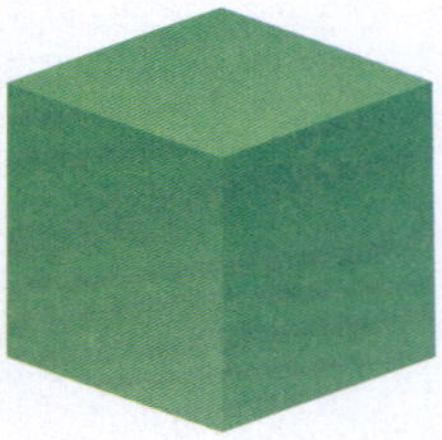 sphere

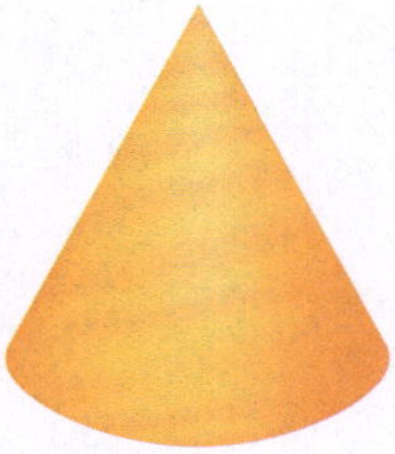 cube

Trace the words, then colour the 3D shapes.

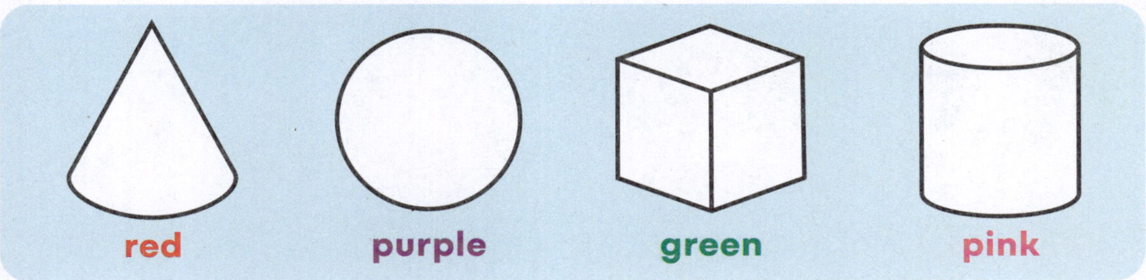

cone sphere cube cylinder

A flat (2D) shape only has length and width. A 3D shape has length, width, and depth.

Continue each pattern.

Fill in the missing parts of the pattern.

Now make your own.

Fractions

A fraction is a part of a whole. It tells us how many parts we have from a total number of equal parts.

Colour $\frac{1}{2}$.

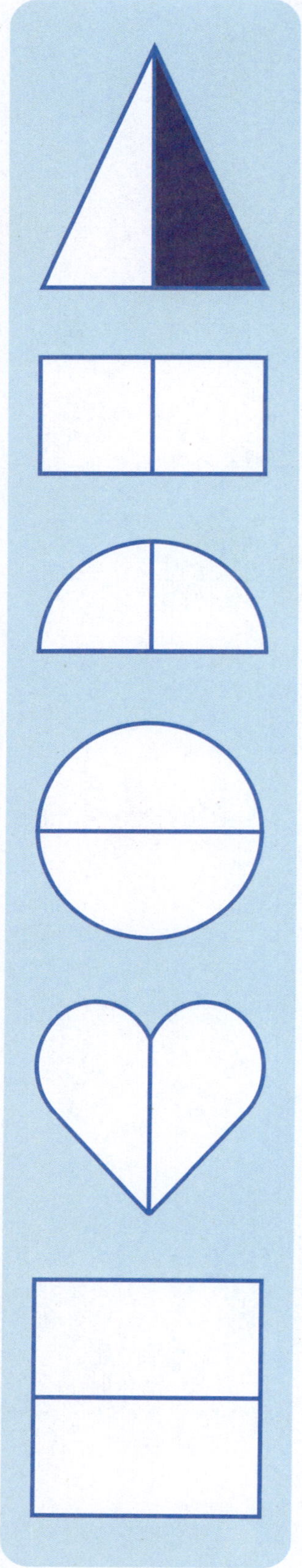

Colour $\frac{1}{3}$.

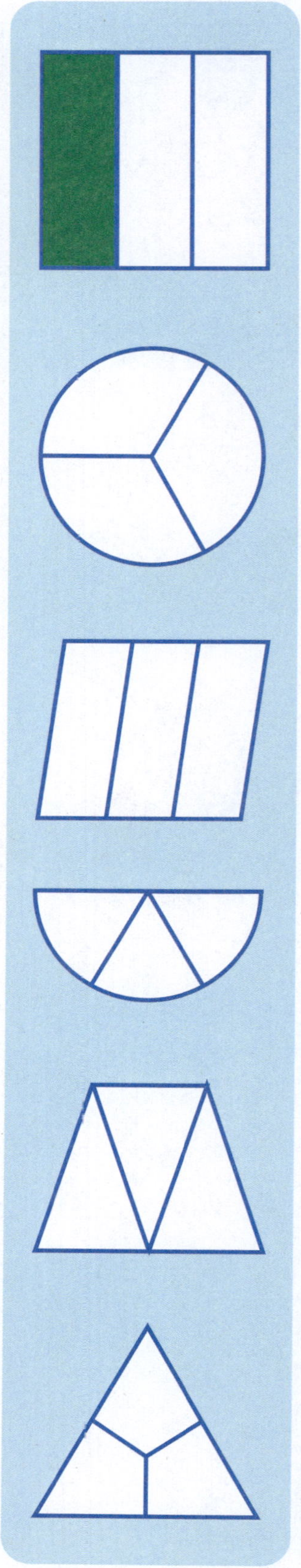

Colour $\frac{2}{3}$.

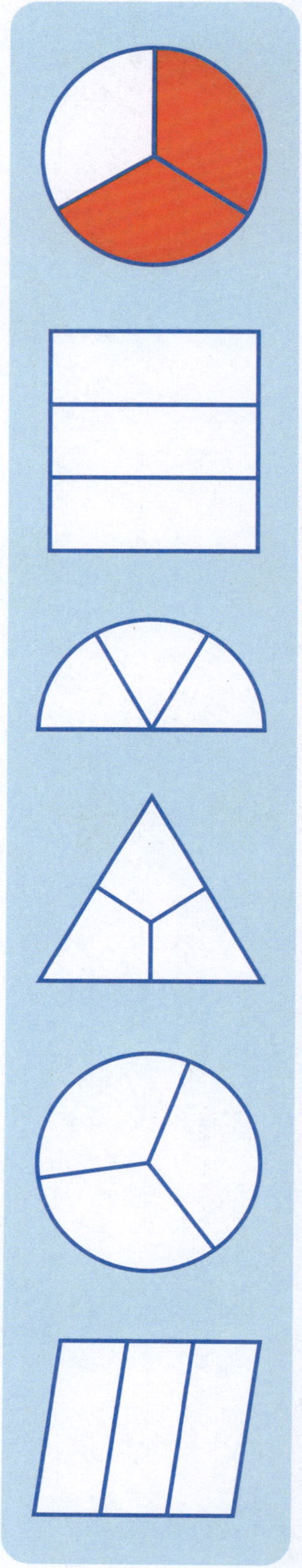

Colour $\frac{1}{4}$.

Colour $\frac{3}{4}$.

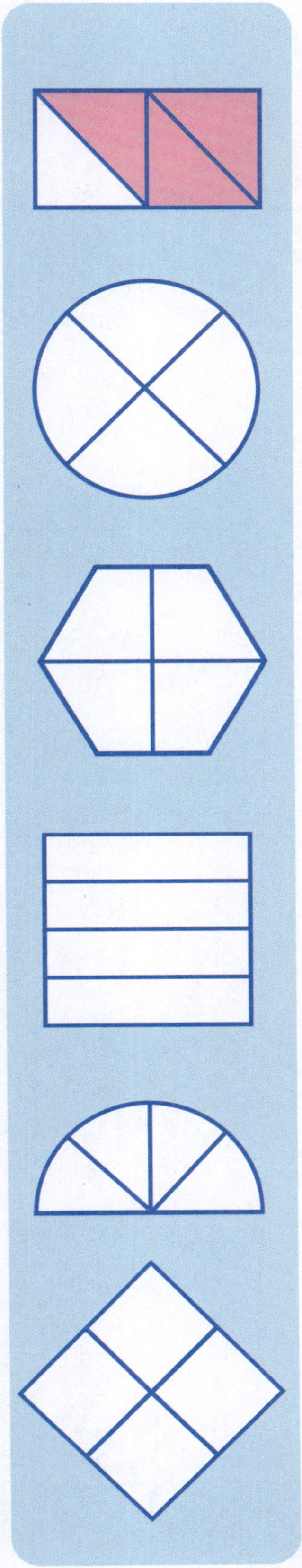

Slices of pizza are an example of fractions! If a pizza has **4** slices, and we take only **1** slice, we have **1/4** (one quarter) of a pizza.

What fraction of the pizza would we have if we took **3** slices? What if we took **2** slices?

Fractions

Put a check mark beside the fraction that represents the shaded area of each shape.

○ $\frac{1}{2}$ ○ $\frac{3}{4}$ ○ $\frac{1}{4}$ ○ $\frac{1}{3}$

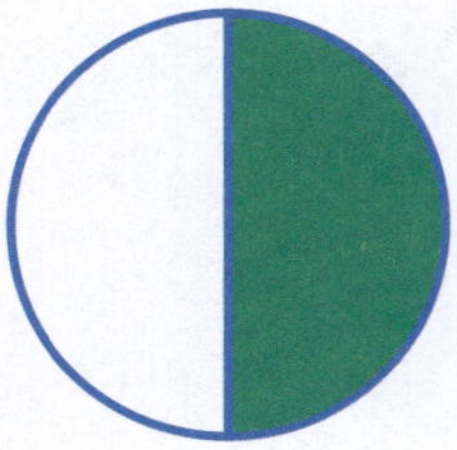

○ $\frac{2}{3}$ ○ $\frac{2}{4}$ ○ $\frac{1}{4}$ ○ $\frac{1}{2}$

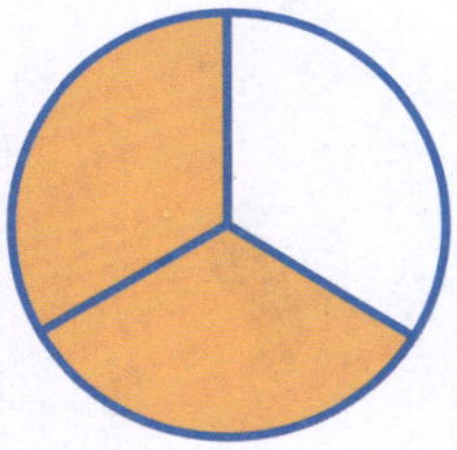

○ $\frac{3}{4}$ ○ $\frac{1}{2}$ ○ $\frac{2}{3}$ ○ $\frac{1}{3}$

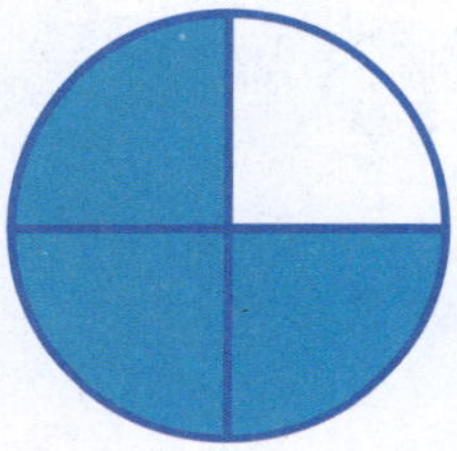

○ $\frac{2}{3}$ ○ $\frac{3}{4}$ ○ $\frac{1}{2}$ ○ $\frac{1}{4}$

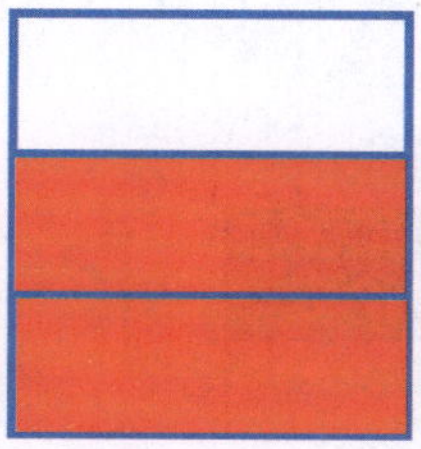

○ $\frac{1}{2}$ ○ $\frac{3}{4}$ ○ $\frac{1}{4}$ ○ $\frac{2}{3}$

○ $\frac{2}{3}$ ○ $\frac{2}{4}$ ○ $\frac{1}{4}$ ○ $\frac{1}{2}$

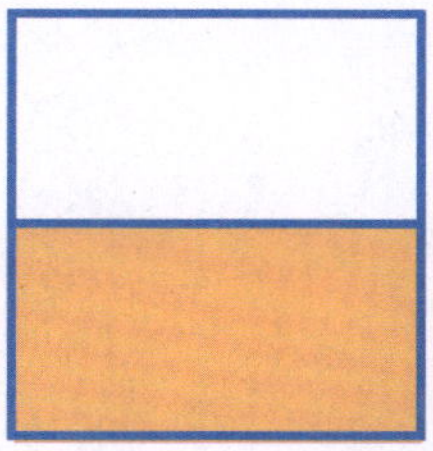

○ $\frac{3}{4}$ ○ $\frac{1}{2}$ ○ $\frac{2}{3}$ ○ $\frac{1}{3}$

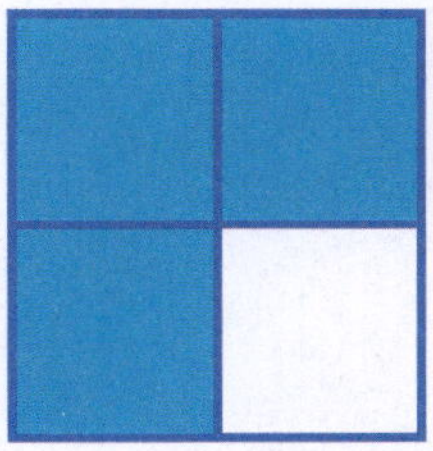

○ $\frac{2}{4}$ ○ $\frac{1}{3}$ ○ $\frac{1}{4}$ ○ $\frac{3}{4}$

Look at the pictograph and answer the questions below.

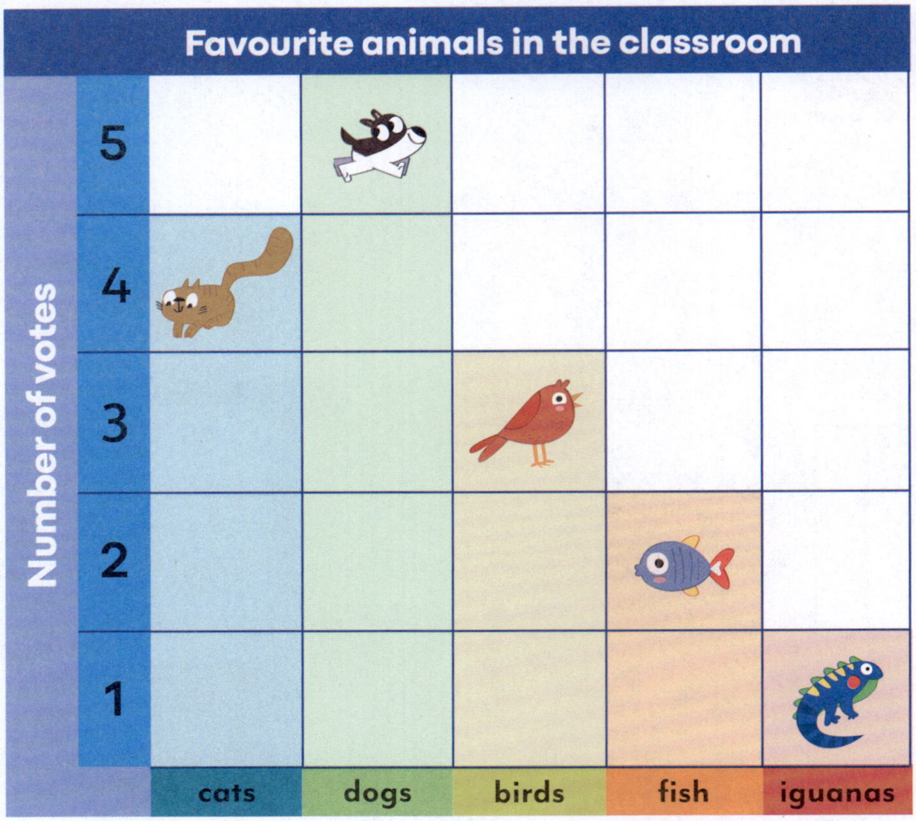

How many students like birds best? ☐

How many students like cats best? ☐

How many more students like cats than like iguanas? ☐

Circle the most popular animal in the classroom.

Look at the pictograph and answer the questions below.

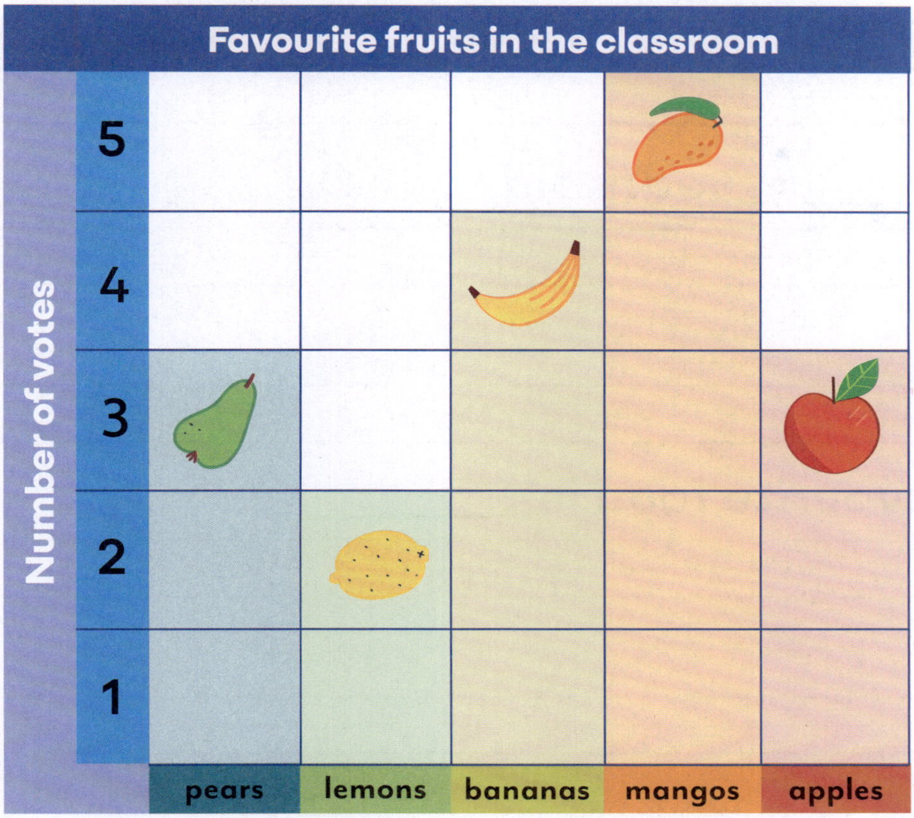

How many students like bananas best? ☐

How many students like apples best? ☐

What fruits are liked equally? ____________________

Circle the most popular fruit in the classroom.

Extra Practice

Copy these phrases and fill in the blanks.

My name is ______.

My name is ______.

I am ______ years old.

I am ______ years old.

I live in ______.

I live in ______.

My favourite food is ______.

I favourite food is ______.

You can write other facts about yourself on the empty lines.

Try writing your own sentences about other things you like or the people in your life.

Extra Practice

Draw your own patterns using shapes.

Draw a scene using only geometric shapes.

Extra Practice

If you can't think of something to draw, try one of these ideas:

- A house, castle, or other building
- A car, train, or truck
- A city or town

Answers

2

My grandma comes for dinner every Sunday.

Sarah has an older brother.

The girl is wearing a green dress.

The alpaca lives in the mountains.

My cat sleeps on my bed.

The parrot has colourful feathers.

3

Bears and deer live in the forest.

There are many planets in space.

We took a boat to the island.

The astronaut flies in a rocket.

I like to put jam on my toast.

I got a balloon at the carnival.

4

Person	Animal
doctor	mouse
sister	pig
uncle	turtle

Place	Thing
beach	book
school	glass
store	grape

5

(circled: bee, cans, plant, pencils, bag, stars)

6

ottawa	canada
Ottawa	Canada
asia	jupiter
Asia	Jupiter
christina	mr. cruz
Christina	Mr. Cruz

8

the lake. (thumbs down)

and walk to it. (thumbs down)

The car is red. (thumbs up)

She put down the. (thumbs down)

We had fun. (thumbs up)

9

Fred and Lora are — growing strawberries.

Their greenhouse is — large.

Fred waters — the plants.

Lora picks the — berries.

They work — together.

The strawberries — are red.

10

My name is Bob.

I am an astronaut.

Answers

11

I have a cool robot.

I explore planets.

Time to fly!

12

where is my backpack
Where is my backpack?

did Sherin bring the basketball
Did Sherin bring the basketball?

when does class start
When does class start?

what month is it
What month is it?

how does it work
How does it work?

13

I forgot my lunch box.	[thumbs down circled]
Can I play with you?	[thumbs up circled]
The bicycle is purple.	[thumbs down circled]
What did they say?	[thumbs up circled]
Are you hungry?	[thumbs up circled]
I am feeling sick.	[thumbs down circled]
Can we keep it?	[thumbs up circled]

14

I do not like mushrooms.	[thumbs down circled]
Did you drink water?	[thumbs down circled]
The movie was so cool!	[thumbs up circled]
He ate the last piece!	[thumbs up circled]

15

that car is so fast
That car is so fast!

she's the winner
She's the winner!

wow, that's beautiful
Wow, that's beautiful!

ah, there's a spider
Ah, there's a spider!

i can't wait
I can't wait!

i forgot my bag
I forgot my bag!

16

we went on a trip to ontario.
We went on a trip to Ontario.

ana is from mexico.
Ana is from Mexico.

bree and kai played jenga.
Bree and Kai played Jenga.

i like eating at taco bell.
I like eating at Taco Bell.

we camped in banff park.
We camped in Banff Park.

jane and i shop at costco.
Jane and I shop at Costco.

17

Holidays	Months of the Year	Days of the Week
Easter	January	Monday
Labour Day	June	Tuesday

this wednesday is christmas!
This Wednesday is Christmas!

my birthday is august 16.
My birthday is August 16.

i have art class on tuesday.
I have art class on Tuesday.

18

When did Peter arrive ?

Jen planted seeds in the garden .

Would you like to play with me ?

I wore my new shoes to school .

Yay! Mikayla brought cake !

We're going to be late !

Answers

19

Brianna, Jeremy, and Lily are my cousins.
My favourite hobbies are drawing, playing football, and swimming.
I have hockey practice on Monday, Wednesday, and Friday.
I used green, blue, and yellow crayons to draw.
Do you want chocolate, vanilla, or strawberry ice cream?
I want pepperoni, cheese, and peppers on my pizza.
We are travelling to Toronto, Ottawa, and Montreal.
I live with my mom, my dad, and my sister.

20

read	bucket	dance	cute	paper	talk
pink	swim	blue	car	run	play
Bailey	eye	climb	mouse	sing	why

Katie eats her ice cream.

I ride my bicycle.

Victor dives into the pool.

21

The kids play together.

Anna gives Max her bunny.

He loves his toy car.

They make a mess.

Anna and Max draw.

22

Last year, I won the science fair.
My family walked in the park.
The cat is snuggled in its bed.
The mug is full of tea.
Walter went to the movies.

23

Hugo walks his dog.

The birds sing.

The twins love to read.

Emma waters the flowers.

24

Steven and Mike	we
the boy	it
the cat	he
Diana and I	they
The girls	he
Sally	we
Alan	it
The chair	you
You and I	they
You and Aileen	she

25

The popsicle is cold.

The panda is fluffy.

I love my new bicycle helmet.

The peanuts are salty and crunchy.

26

red

blue

orange

purple

yellow

black

green

brown

27

F	R	O	M	M	A	N	Y	H	I
W	K	W	I	E	B	N	I	E	V
O	M	I	F	A	O	C	V	L	F
A	F	T	E	R	U	U	E	P	W
J	B	H	L	T	T	P	L	A	Y
E	H	D	O	A	R	O	V	S	T
V	X	J	S	U	U	B	R	K	H
E	H	E	R	E	C	G	M	W	E
R	T	W	G	J	D	O	W	N	I
Y	C	O	U	L	D	P	W	Y	R

28

Y	A	H	J	N	W	C	N	F	P	D
D	X	P	Z	J	P	I	B	O	O	T
Y	Z	D	W	H	C	O	I	R	C	X
E	P	W	F	U	A	X	P	K	U	P
Y	A	L	S	J	T	A	B	L	E	O
V	N	M	D	S	S	P	O	O	N	T
P	C	H	A	I	R	P	N	C	U	P
G	T	R	T	N	S	R	V	U	M	I
B	O	W	L	K	D	P	E	R	N	T

29

A	I	D	T	U	P	V	V	R	M	X
R	T	V	G	T	M	N	E	D	D	P
B	R	O	W	N	R	U	J	U	C	U
L	M	N	G	R	E	E	N	Y	O	R
A	S	W	G	S	I	Y	O	U	R	P
C	B	Y	E	L	L	O	W	R	A	L
K	L	H	S	U	Z	O	E	B	N	E
D	U	P	I	N	K	L	H	Q	G	X
R	E	D	E	H	P	G	J	X	E	W

30

E	H	K	U	W	U	X	U	Z	Q	B
K	J	R	G	A	X	M	T	C	A	T
A	H	B	E	F	G	T	B	O	O	T
F	D	B	V	B	I	R	D	W	D	T
G	V	E	D	Z	F	W	P	F	U	U
K	I	A	E	F	I	S	H	P	C	T
V	O	R	B	I	Z	Z	Y	D	K	X
M	H	L	G	L	I	O	N	H	S	V
K	O	A	L	A	F	Q	C	D	O	G

31

K	Q	C	Q	B	I	K	E	H	Y	Z
X	P	C	W	Q	P	K	C	J	S	T
T	R	A	I	N	Z	L	P	S	C	M
X	T	F	L	L	L	A	L	V	O	C
T	R	U	C	K	B	C	A	R	O	S
P	F	H	T	E	O	V	N	W	T	B
M	E	T	F	F	A	Q	E	S	E	U
V	E	Y	P	X	T	Y	L	Q	R	S
O	T	F	H	V	O	J	O	Y	B	P

32

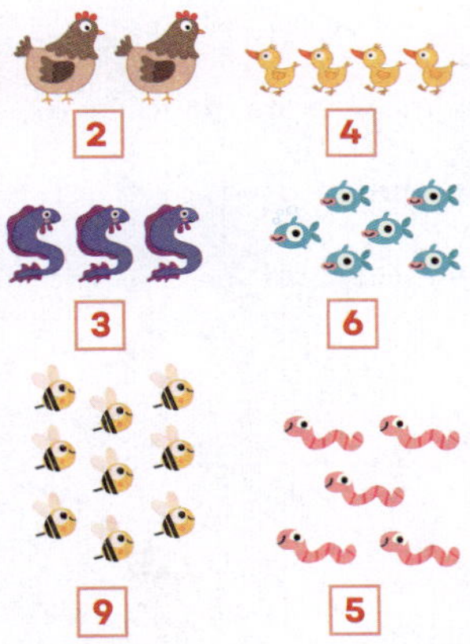

33

five

nine

three

one

34

35

(11) 13 15 — 17 10 (12)

10 (16) 13 — 15 20 (18)

36

14	ten
2	seven
10	fourteen
12	eight
20	sixteen
7	two
16	twenty
11	twelve
8	eleven

37

twelve	21	12	twenty	20	√
seventeen	17	√	nine	9	√
ten	1	10	sixteen	61	16
eleven	11	√	nineteen	91	19
eighteen	81	18	fourteen	14	√

1 2 — 13 14 — 8 9

24 25 — 22 23 — 29 30

35 36 37 — 43 44 45

48 49 50 — 22 23 24

38

39

How many eyes do you see? 29

How many frames? 9

How many stars? 15

40

How many balloons do you see? 9

How many stars? 15

How many hearts? 10

41

42

1 + 5 = 6

5 + 5 = 10

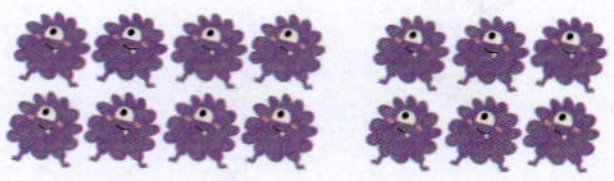

8 + 6 = 14

Answers

43

9 + 9 = 18

1 + 5 = 6	5 + 5 = 10	8 + 6 = 14	9 + 9 = 18

44

4 + 4 = 8

4 + 2 = 6

3 + 6 = 9

9 + 4 = 13

45

4 + 4 = 8	4 + 2 = 6	3 + 6 = 9	9 + 4 = 13

46

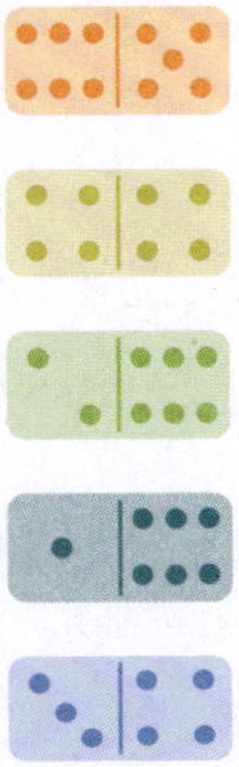

6 + 5 = 11

4 + 4 = 8

2 + 6 = 8

1 + 6 = 7

3 + 4 = 7

47

3 + 6 = 9	4 + 2 = 6	5 + 2 = 7
4 + 6 = 10	3 + 3 = 6	
6 + 6 = 12	1 + 5 = 6	

48

1 + 1 = 2	1 + 9 = 10
1 + 2 = 3	1 + 10 = 11
1 + 3 = 4	2 + 1 = 3
1 + 4 = 5	2 + 2 = 4
1 + 5 = 6	2 + 3 = 5
1 + 6 = 7	2 + 4 = 6
1 + 7 = 8	2 + 5 = 7
1 + 8 = 9	2 + 6 = 8

49

2 + 7 = 9	2 + 8 = 10	2 + 9 = 11	10 + 10 = 20	3 + 3 = 6
4 + 3 = 7	5 + 3 = 8	6 + 3 = 9	7 + 3 = 10	8 + 3 = 11
10 + 4 = 14	8 + 4 = 12	6 + 4 = 10	4 + 4 = 8	7 + 4 = 11
9 + 4 = 13	8 + 4 = 12	7 + 9 = 16	6 + 10 = 16	10 + 3 = 13

50

16 - 4 = 12

12 - 4 = 8

14 - 8 = 6

Answers

51

16	12	14
- 4	- 4	- 8
12	8	6

52

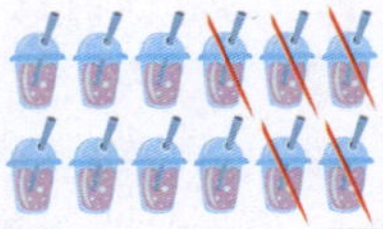

12 - 5 = 7

20 - 6 = 14

16 - 6 = 10

53

12	20	16
- 5	- 6	- 6
7	14	10

54

6 - 5 = 1

4 - 4 = 0

6 - 4 = 2

5 - 4 = 1

6 - 2 = 4

55

3	4	5	6	3	4	4
- 2	- 2	- 2	- 2	- 3	- 3	- 4
1	2	3	4	0	1	0

56

6 - 1 = 5	10 - 3 = 7
7 - 2 = 5	10 - 6 = 4
8 - 3 = 5	10 - 2 = 8
5 - 4 = 1	10 - 4 = 6
5 - 3 = 2	10 - 1 = 9
9 - 1 = 8	10 - 5 = 5
8 - 2 = 6	10 - 10 = 0
6 - 3 = 3	10 - 0 = 10

57

15 - 8 = 7	15 - 1 = 14	15 - 9 = 6	15 - 3 = 12	15 - 6 = 9
20 - 9 = 11	20 - 2 = 18	20 - 8 = 12	20 - 5 = 15	20 - 10 = 10
18 - 5 = 13	18 - 4 = 14	18 - 3 = 15	18 - 2 = 16	18 - 1 = 17
12 - 7 = 5	16 - 6 = 10	11 - 5 = 6	17 - 4 = 13	19 - 3 = 16

58

60

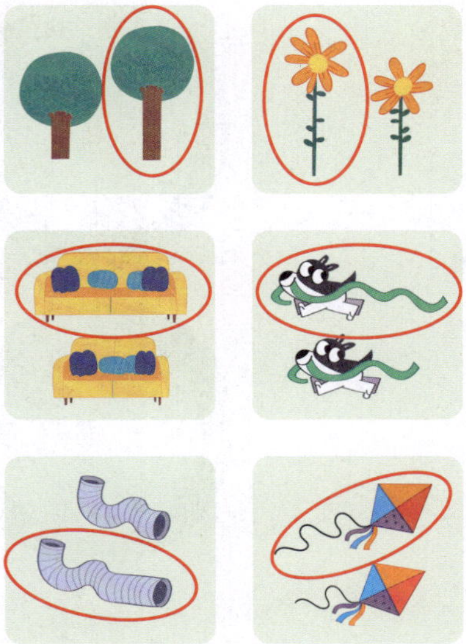

61

62

63

64

65

66

4 o'clock

11 o'clock

7 o'clock

3 o'clock

8 o'clock

5 o'clock

67

8:30

1:30

2:30

5:30

7:30

4:30

68

3:00

11:00

8:00

12:00

6:00

5:00

69

3:30

1:30

8:30

12:30

10:30

5:30

70

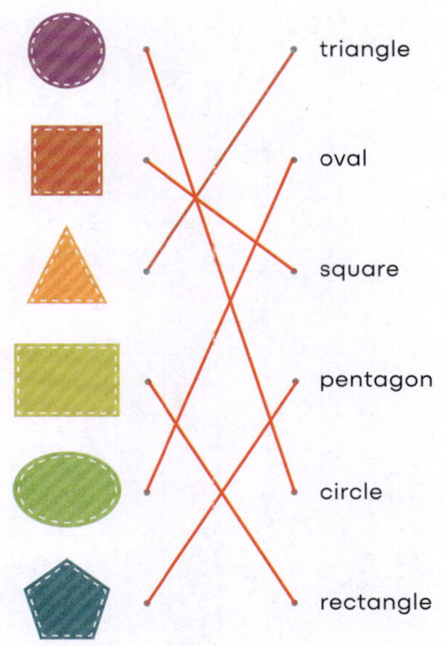

71

72

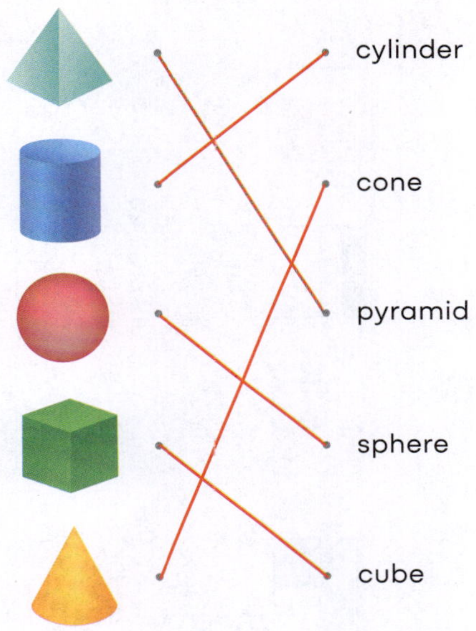

73

74

75

76

77

78

○ $\frac{1}{2}$ ○ $\frac{3}{4}$ ✓ $\frac{1}{4}$ ○ $\frac{1}{3}$

○ $\frac{2}{3}$ ○ $\frac{2}{4}$ ○ $\frac{1}{4}$ ✓ $\frac{1}{2}$

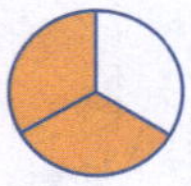
○ $\frac{3}{4}$ ○ $\frac{1}{2}$ ✓ $\frac{2}{3}$ ○ $\frac{1}{3}$

○ $\frac{2}{3}$ ✓ $\frac{3}{4}$ ○ $\frac{1}{2}$ ○ $\frac{1}{4}$

79

○ $\frac{1}{2}$ ○ $\frac{3}{4}$ ○ $\frac{1}{4}$ ✓ $\frac{2}{3}$

○ $\frac{2}{3}$ ○ $\frac{2}{4}$ ✓ $\frac{1}{4}$ ○ $\frac{1}{2}$

○ $\frac{3}{4}$ ✓ $\frac{1}{2}$ ○ $\frac{2}{3}$ ○ $\frac{1}{3}$

○ $\frac{2}{4}$ ○ $\frac{1}{3}$ ○ $\frac{1}{4}$ ✓ $\frac{3}{4}$

80

How many students like birds best? **3**

How many students like cats best? **4**

How many more students like cats than like iguanas? **3**

81

How many students like bananas best? **4**

How many students like apples best? **3**

What fruits are liked equally? pears apples

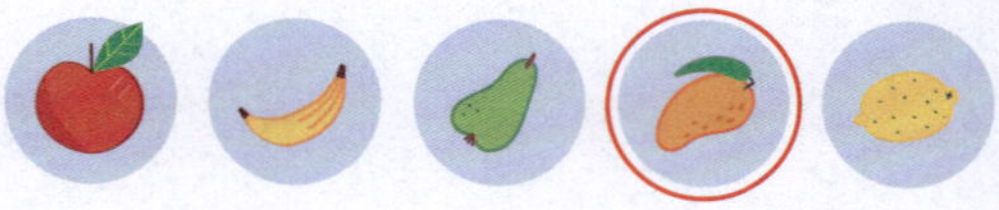